new 85 rep

W9-CIG-045

CARROLL & GRAF PUBLISHERS, INC.

New York

OWL

Drawings by Walter Richards

William Service

Carroll & Graf Publishers, inc.
New York

Copyright © 1969 by William Service

Part of this book appeared in *Sports Illustrated* before publication.

"I Am Rose" by Gertrude Stein from THE WORLD IS ROUND, is reprinted by permission of the publishers, William R. Scott, Inc. Copyright renewed © 1967 by Daniel C. Joseph Admr. d.b.n. CTA of the Estate of Gertrude Stein.

Reprinted by arrangement with Alfred A. Knopf, Inc.

All rights reserved. No part of this book may be reproduced in any form or by any means without the written permission of the publisher.

First Carroll & Graf Edition 1985

Carroll & Graf Publishers, Inc.
260 Fifth Avenue
New York, N.Y. 10001

ISBN: 0-88184-120-X

Manufactured in the United States of America

To Lia, Will, Grant, Timmy, Martha,

and Jason and Claggart

OWL

Owl

. . . slides his foot down the curve of the fire screen, then, bobbing and swinging his head to get the range, he eases his weight forward onto that foot. The off-leg stays angled behind him. He sights in again on the tomcat, who half dozes six feet away. Owl makes tiny adjustments, leans still farther forward. But no attack occurs, and there he is simply perched on the fire screen again: Owl's life is full of such empty melodrama. Since many of his hours are passed each day in gray, rather scruffy inaction, in being the half-interested observer of a great many commotions of no relevance to his life, and since each day is spent under the strictest house arrest, perhaps he needs to exaggerate his excitements. Or it may be that, against some grayness in our own lives, we are the ones who exaggerate.

An owl is an odd creature to keep about the house. Also for forest, hedgerow, meadow to keep. An odd creature anywhere.

I would like to describe how I removed the bird from the nest of its parents, senselessly shot, the nest in a cavity high up in a dead tree too rotten to climb:

the traverse rope between two adjacent hickories*
hand-over-hand until directly above the nest, and so
forth. What happened was, our retriever puppy discovered the fuzzball, beaky and glare-eyed, in woods
behind the house, and bellowed at it until children
came. They brought it home in a coffee can, and piped
the usual question. "Go home, Owl," I wanted to say,
but the woods borders are a cruel territory for anything odd and defenseless. Dogs, cats, children patrol
steadily. He had been brought to a house already beset
with enough and too many animals: the obligatory dog
and cat, a big aquarium, half a dozen assorted turtles,
two wild ducklings whose history began like Owl's, a
domestic squirrel on board while the owners vacation.
(Our youngest, Grant, has reminded me—three cups
of dust in which his antlions lived.) But especially I
wanted no more of foundling birds. Their demands
are greater than those of all the others put together.
Most of them require much expertise. Our usual
experience has been, they eat ravenously awhile, and
then die.

Owl kept up a continuous chirring noise, soft and
scratchy. The yellow binocular stare from out of the
coffee can seemed to return my own stare, but not so;
I moved out of line and the eyes did not waver. The
owlet stood on its own two feet, looking alert and

* The locally common mockernut hickory, *Carya tomentosa*.

4

fearless. *Feed* him. The only fare immediately available was some soaked dog meal, pretty humble stuff. I offered a chunk, which Owl ignored until it touched the bristles beside his beak; then with a garble noise he seized it and gulped it down. Behind that little hooked beak there gapes a surprising width of mouth. He snatched another chunk, uttered his noise. All right, we keep him. To register the new citizen, I looked him up in the guide. I announced rather hastily that we had a barred owl, *Strix varia*. Later that day, a suggestion of tufts perking up for "horns." A closer look. *Otus asio*, the screech owl.

Anthropomorphize Owl

. . . it is going to be impossible not to. He postures too much; he walks about bobbing like an old man with hands clasped behind back. He looks one in the eye, with furious intent. He gazes wistfully out the window into the woodland home he may or may not ever haunt again. He pulls my ear affectionately. On the other hand, much of the time it is impossible to make even that kind of sense out of what he is doing. He swoops into the philodendron, one after the other snips three leaves, which he then ignores. He perches in the aloe, exclusively crackles off just the dead fronds. Next time, he will nibble just the green ones. My daughter and a friend were playing a board game: Owl swept away with a man. What are you *doing,* Owl? As I read, he may perch on my knee. Is he sitting on my knee, or is he perched on a limb which happens to be my knee? First, let's go back and raise our owl.

Fledgling Owl
Easy to House, Feed

. . . except that he never stayed fed very long, and soon got the urge to march about. Owl took from three to twelve meals a day: it depends whether you consider one cricket delivered in a child's fist a formal meal. Even so, owl parents can call themselves lucky, their feedings have more substance and are processed much more slowly than the pap of insects and berries given other nestlings. The five foster parents marched a doomed procession of moths and beetles and crickets and grasshoppers down that throat, plus squads of what one interested woman termed "Bill's artificial animals": bits of beef liver wrapped in cat hair; chicken gizzard in poodle fur;

dog food, bristly as any caterpillar, with a coat of human hair; feathered shrimp. These last represented almost all I knew about owls: that their digestive tracts require the roughage. For some weeks, Owl refused hamburger. (Did he know something about hamburger we didn't know?) What does an owl do when he refuses food? He draws himself to his full height, tucks his beak into his chest feathers, and stiff-legged backs away, glaring. If one presses the food on him, his horns go up.

Owl Eyes

... when they shut, Owl has very nearly achieved the childhood fantasy, that when you shut your eyes no one can see you.

Owl, now full-grown, has an optical system remarkable both for its capacities and its limitations. In the dimmest light, he spots out of the corner of his eye, from perhaps twenty feet away, a small moth dropped to the floor, and the only reason I know it's there is because I dropped it for him. Yet, as long as it doesn't move, he is weak at registering prey by its form and color alone: a fat moth on the wall may well be ignored. Unless Owl is very hungry, in which case he prowls and scans his familiar world for *something suspicious,* and any foreign shape is then recorded in many perspectives if it looks even remotely like food. His decision is usually correct. In consequence, Owl seems avid to see. A full belly cannot still that visual appetite completely. To pick out an important "event" (which, again, may be perfectly unmoving), Owl must first learn the background in detail. He has learned what a bare plate looks like, and lets it pass. Because much of his food is sawed from some frozen chunk and left to thaw on a plate, Owl has deduced—or perhaps he is merely playing the probabilities—that any lump of a thing on a plate is owl food. Quite likely he will strike, or at least approach to investigate. And so we often see Owl, by our exquisite standards, making a fool of himself over a cigarette butt or bread crust against the background of a plate. In dim light, the human pupil can be seen to dilate smoothly; Owl's snaps open immediately to what must be twice the area of the human, then may shutter right down again to the proverbial pinpoint. The two extremes represent maximum sensitivity at "open" and maximum sharpness of image at "closed," and any time Owl sights in on something of unusual interest he will use two f-stops, his pupils so fast they seem to blink.

Owl the far-seer . . . conversely, anything closer than eight or ten inches he can scarcely see at all, which means that he can form no useful image of what

he holds in his talons. And now I can offer two possible reasons for Owl's odd habit of closing his eyes when he eats. First, he can't really see what he's got, so why not? Second, the things he eats some of them are known to thrash around a little, who wants that in the eye? Does he *think* to guard his eyes, or is it automatic? Since they also close when he drinks water, let's call it automatic, without being perfectly sure what automatic means.

Sagacious Owl, bird of Athene, goddess of wisdom —he can't even see his own feet. Nor can his eyes move in their sockets. Owl's eyelids can come up from the bottom as well as down from the top, also sometimes the upper ones come down on the bias; now he looks sleepy, Oriental, wise, in a minute he may look cross-eyed, but the books are right, an owl cannot move his eyes. If we suddenly found ourselves with eyes fixed in our heads, we would be plagued with double vision. Our eyes have to converge on something to focus. Whether Owl's lines of sight "go out" parallel, or converge on some fixed point, well, just how would you go about finding the answer? First of all, there is no reason why effective movement (i.e., navigation) can't be based on double images; as a matter of fact it's the situation in most of the nonhuman vertebrate world. It's not, of course, our situation. When we focus on something with our two eyes, each eye takes the thing in from a slightly different angle and this slight difference in the two images—which become fused into a single Out There—lends depth to the arrangement of things out there and a sense of solidity to the things themselves. It's what we lose when we close one eye. If your eyes never converge on anything, Owl, can you use binocular disparity to help you locate things? No answer, although he emphasizes that for the free owl the judgment of distance is a matter of life and death, period. But Owl's practice tells us something more. He reacts to a strange environment, or to something strange in a familiar environment, by bobbing and swinging his head: up-down-side-to-side-diagonally: children imitate him a lot better than I can describe. As a novice flyer, Owl would hardly ever take off without considerable head movement. As an adult, he still makes a subtle check. As Owl moves his head about, the way things Out There seem to move in relation to each other gives clues as to how near or far they are. What is the term for that process? *Motion parallax.*

And now, a little experiment you can work with your own or a borrowed screech owl. First, place him on your hand about eighteen inches from your face. Get him so he's looking you square in the eye. Now, before he turns his attention to something else, move the hand under him in slow circles, back-forth, up-down, etc. Note what your owl does, and we'll discuss it later.

Growing Up to Become an Owl

. . . the odds are against the success of even an owlet. A major factor is the development of that optical system. At first only the motion of large objects would attract his attention, and not dependably. Soon, however, he began to try to sight in on things with the swing and bob of head so characteristic of him. Functionally, nevertheless, he was blind. He had been living contentedly in his coffee can on a shelf, never going more than a few feet from its entrance. To show him off to a friend who was at supper with us, we set the owlet on the table with dessert. He marched, hip-hop, across the table, up one side of the guest's ice cream and down the other (who said something in a resigned tone of voice, and smoothed the prints out of his ice cream) and continued his way off the edge of the table. He took four falls this way, until finally he learned how an edge looks. "Now we know how he fell out of the nest," our guest observed.

"Or else his mother kicked him out because he's an imbecile."

Grounded, the flightless owlet never showed the slightest fear of anything. Slow afoot, too weak to defend himself, for a wild creature rather strong-smelling,* of what use fear? The grounded owlet, if an orphan, has one resource: face. And so he presented beak and furious yellow stare face-on to anything that approached, and went *chirr* at it. The animal which looks back at you with two eyes at once tends to stand high in the local food chain, i.e., not one of nature's victims. Our prodigious puppy Jason, the one who found Owl in the first place, likes to take small animals and the wrists of children in his great soft mouth and march about (an escaped wild duckling got a fair tour of the neighborhood that way, was recovered unhurt but very soggy) but has pushed no such familiarity on Owl, fledgling or mature.

It has been reported that many owl fledglings leave the nest before they can fly, and are supported as they clamber about on the ground and up trees by the parents—air support for the ground forces. It seems a chancy way to raise children, yet there are new owls every year so it must work. Our fledgling stayed near the mouth of his coffee can for about a week†; but

---

* An owl smells about the way you would expect an owl to smell, perhaps somewhat better; far milder than, say, long-haired dog, mole, tomcat, or ant, or person.

† Where a visitor recognized him immediately: "It's People-are-no-damn-good!" The Steig cartoon.

then, long before he could fly, he set out into the world on foot—a world which he could scarcely see, which would have to be worked into shape through trial and error, and which he could not hope to exploit for food. The child leaving home with his clothes and a favorite toy in a bag tied to a stick is better equipped to make a living. Nevertheless off Owl went presumably coded with the knowledge that his parents were maintaining overflights, and gave the evil eye, the HEX, to whatever came his way. The hex works on the cat, who has never granted amnesty to any other weaker household creature luckless enough to go before him. (The cat's name is Harold Claggart, and he says, "It is regrettable that the prisoner was deceased in an attempt to escape from confinement," in chill officialese.) Claggart is an expert on other animals. Some dogs he flees, some he ignores, some he fights, others he keeps so far away from he never *has* to fight or flee. No great hunter, only lust and combat truly stir him; nevertheless he knows how to and will kill a chance squirrel or vole or bird, will ignore toad and wasp, will munch a grasshopper. A pragmatist. How does he react to Owl? On introduction, he was curiosity on stiff legs; he advanced his nose carefully, the little owl, shut-eyed, leaned forward and delivered the nibble and buzz he gave everything which came to him. Claggart, not charmed, pulled back. In the next few hours, the two of them defined the poles of their relationship which still stand: mild aversion, indifference, and that instinctive flicker from eye to muscle, muscle to claw, or eye to gland and back to eye, or whatever and around and around, which I will call curiosity. Two rival gangs have agreed to a truce but the gunmen are a bit edgy, that's what Owl and Claggart remind me of, and their few face-to-face encounters are from the same movie. . . .

Owl, under a protective umbrella of parents, firing his hex in all directions, was exploring on foot. Still flightless, he had just learned to pounce* and saw in front of him the twitching tail of the sleeping cat. He pounced on the twitch. Infantile as the bird was, beak and talons were still needly, and the cat must have felt each one. In cartoons, a cat so attacked goes straight up in the air, his mouth open yowling, his hair electrically bristling. Claggart—to get it as accurately as possible, I will drop in the phrase—got hastily to his feet. A standard cat posture: arched and twisted body, ears back, a nasty show of teeth, the weight shifted off one front leg which makes a menacing half-movement: it's a movie again, the bully who is really a coward and

---

* Let's say "learned" to pounce; maturation was required as well as study. For a couple of weeks he did not pounce at all, and then one evening he pounced on a beetle 100 per cent. The transition was the short two-legged hop he would make in getting from place to place; it remained only to link that hop onto moving target.

is not going to fight it out instead sneers and snarls out of it as best he can. The tail having whipped out of his clutch, Owl had made some kind of retreat but was still staring at what was looming up in front of him. You can say he was aware of the magnitude of his error but was brazening it out, or you can say he was staring aghast at the consequences of his act. Claggart slouched off and lay down again. I insist on the strangeness of the cat's reactions. He lightly spikes people who get too cuddly with him. He has finally come to allow Jason to nuzzle him, but he spikes him for any too-sudden or buffoonish approach. My mother-in law's black poodle can bark and harass until she actually arrives on the cat, then he spikes her. And although Claggart was watched, spied upon every instant he was with the young owl, he has never been seen to make a threatening move; nor has he ever been hit or yelled at when near the owl, which might instill some kind of fear of the bird. In a similar procedure, I put Claggart and a visiting hamster together, free. The cat may have been about to go for it, but he was easily soothed back into mere watchfulness and then indifference. That was the night that the same hamster squeezed out of its cage and was killed by the same cat. It is not mildness which keeps Claggart in his place, nor is it fear of or loyalty to the household gods. I don't know what it is. It is the HEX.

What enters the mind of a fifty-pound golden retriever puppy when confronted with maybe four ounces of owl? Much of that "mind" is nose, and so he thinks to extend his broad velvety nose further and further toward Owl, trying to define what is there. As usual, Owl goes *chirr* and nibbles the nose. Prodigiously excited, Jason curvets, bows, waves his tail like a banner, paws the floor: the invitation to the romp. There is real danger that Owl will simply be stepped on, and he is removed.

For many days Owl only stared at insects set free in front of him: they might draw his attention, but then they could walk right out of his unswerving field of vision. Then he began to track them with an amazed, furious glare. Then one evening, so young that his flights were mostly jump, Owl, strutting about on a sofa, was presented with a large, slow beetle. He strained himself up to full height, studied down his chest at the beetle, backed off, bobbed a few times, then hopped right on target. As if seeking approbation, Owl glanced up. Or perhaps he needed instructions. The beetle emerged from the thicket of talons, seeming to proceed on knees and elbows. As has been pointed out, Owl is farsighted, in the weakest sense of the term. Where is the beetle, where did he go? Hop-hop back, and another pounce. Again the beetle worked his way past the beak and talons. And repeat, until we realized the armor was proof against the owlet's beak.

In gradual increments, Owl learns to see, to fly, to pounce and kill. He sees the figured curtain to be a tangle of vines, and he will climb them, almost upside down, clinging by talon and hook of beak, wings beating. After two or three ascents, it is too much trouble for him to prove he is right; he gives up on the curtain. He sees that any flat, unfigured surface (door, cornice, plaster wall) is open air, and he flies into the face of fact. Well, so things are in the forest, and the owl's eye is born knowing it, long before the wings act on that knowledge. In our house, three or four cracks against such "open air" undo this dogma of the genes. Glass is a special case, since nearly every pane is in front of a screen, which he acutely registers as a barrier. When he tries to land on the screen, he bounces obliquely from the glass. Several times. Much range-sensing from the security of a chair back. He tries to land on a mullion, which is almost but not quite possible. Trying again, he lands on a sill or transom. One or two more mistakes, and the lesson is learned. Soon we will see him with forehead pressed lightly against the glass, looking out.

Incident

The young Owl did not chalk up the number of insect "kills" to his credit on his fuselage—kept them inside—but if he had, the number that evening would have been less than twenty. A novice owl. He was perched on the door chimes. Overhead, just below the ceiling, a big moth, one of the heavy-bodied sort which he especially enjoys, clung to the wall. Not trusting his eyes at such short range, Owl thrust his beak up toward it, several inches short. A nice problem: he cannot pounce upward from where he is, and because of the ceiling he cannot swoop. Owl flew immediately to a perch on a door, turned around to re-sight, and kicked off. Sweeping in through a very acute angle to the wall, at conflux with the moth he did a half-roll and took it in a fine one-handed catch. Well done, Owl!

First Word

. . . the others, the eight distinct vocalizations of Owl, I can more or less imitate, but that nearly incessant *chirr* the infant and then novice Owl made, it defies me. Get a smallish rusty electric motor attached to nothing, plug it in, quickly pull the plug out: it will sound only approximately like the owlet, but you will understand why the noise is hard to imitate. One of life's minute pleasures is to hear his *chirrs* become softer . . . softer . . . he sinks into sleep. Awake, he is like some infernal sending device used by the FBI, he never lets up.* In the forest wouldn't "others" be alerted to an owlet's presence? Why does he keep broadcasting? He is saying, "Here I am, Mother." And since his present "mother" weighs more than two dogs and two cats put together, it is of advantage to him if Mother knows where he is at all times.

Learning to Get Along with Others

. . . trust is involved, but how much trust is appropriate in the life of an owl, free or captive? I think I would say to most owls, "Never trust a cat." Yet Owl is safe in trusting Claggart. Which, again, is not to say that he likes him.

Owl, as he matures, will be seen to adjust and

---

* That first sound has since been dropped from Owl's vocabulary. The process was gradual. Toward maturity, he would go *chirr* only in reply to my whistle, the one I gave whenever I fed him.

readjust his reactions to the cat. Here is an early encounter. . . . The young Owl, with many of his skills not "in" yet though flighted, was working at a piece of raw chicken neck on the kitchen table. Claggart, fond of chicken neck, sprang lightly to a chair: bird and cat regarded each other, an exchange of exceedingly cold, flat stares. Owl went back to his meal, scarcely looking up when the cat stepped onto the table and circled most circumspectly one time, and then, most gingerly, extended one mittened paw to try to nudge, dab the chicken neck away from Owl. A chittering noise from Owl. A dab again. Suspense. Nearby, a door slammed. Owl flew, Claggart cringed, but in the instant recovered to steal the meat. He does not even know that he lost face in doing so, that a tomcat, a brawler, a killer, was seen having to work up courage before confronting a bird not much heavier than a robin. Bad show, Claggart.

Many people want to pet Owl, which sometimes he likes and sometimes he doesn't. His early way out of too much handling was to squawk and take off. Now, more likely than not, and depending on how well he knows the person, he will simply turn and walk a few feet away. Trust is too strong a word, but he has the expectation that he will not be chased and hugged to death. If it's my wife involved, Owl will most likely get his "huggle" no matter what. From inside the embrace he glares yellow outrage. Or perhaps he has found bliss. He is inscrutable.

For this reason or that, we have at times set Owl down outside, near woods—either too young to fly or in a cage. Owl's little bird friends soon arrive. In my mind, I see them transform the woods into so many ornamented Christmas trees. They fill the air with accusation, threat, alarm, and summons. There aren't all that many of them, come right down to it, but enough for a good protest. I enter it here, that an owl on a stump has many acquaintances but few friends.

Owl and Claggart keep generating border incidents. The cat will eat an insect now and then, I don't know why, nor do I know why, having eaten some few, he doesn't go on to take them regularly. We have analogous yens and preferences, most people: pickles, liver, rhubarb, etc. Claggart may believe they tone up the system. Owl has lost a number of bugs to him, sometimes because Claggart beats Owl to the kill, sometimes because the cat will rush up: Owl flies, jettisoning even that tiny extra weight. (It seems natural and in the order of things for a bird to eat an insect; Claggart munches a crackly grasshopper and we compress our lips. We project ourselves into nature, but not consistently.) But Owl when he might like a little snack of something to eat and Owl *hungry*— two different birds. Appetite not only goads him to go harder, it also sharpens his skills. And one skill, at least, seems to be lacking unless he *is* hungry: tracking. For the contented Owl, out of sight is out of mind. The morsel which I hide, the insect which slips away . . . Well, says Owl, it's just too much trouble, I can't remember anything about it; perhaps something else will be coming along sooner or later. The *hungry* Owl disputes with the carving knife as I saw off a piece of frozen meat, searches, pursues, patrols, and if the meal has escaped into a cranny he watches exits and entrances. Only once that I have seen has he been voracious enough to carry the dispute to the cat. Claggart had pinned and was toying with a big hawk moth, all his own. So much edible commotion was too much to resist. Owl plunged down from the kitchen door, gave the cat a faceful of wind, shadow, and flap—Claggart flinched. Owl missed the moth but stirred it up into one last flight which was to a place on the wall where Owl also arrived a moment later. Bravo, Owl!

Owlishness

"Why, the owl," says son Will seeing him from some odd perspective, "he looks almost like a bird." The owl motif these days, in advertising, decorating, cartoons, and so forth . . . well, I was going to say, has become a fad, but any image which has recurred through well over two thousand years to look out at us from coin, pot, fresco, or necktie deserves a better word than fad. The living owl looks like an exaggeration, an intensification, of what an owl is supposed to look like. He flies and he has feathers, so our Owl must be a bird, but it takes some self-reminding now and then that Owl *is* a bird. On the other hand, he is not the sort of pet to make a person say, Why he's almost human. Almost human . . . a smeary kind of comparison; myself, I avoid it except in reference to this or that person, and once I came out with it while inspecting one of those glass-walled ant cities. Anyway, Owl is almost birdlike, and he's mighty like a gnome.

Owl steals a sock, flaps with it to his high nook on the bookshelf. (You think you're an eagle soaring off with a human baby? No answer.) He is not making a nest, he simply wants the sock, and when it is retaken he clings to it upside down, chittering in rage. Placid now, he likes having his beak rubbed between thumb and forefinger, having his chin chucked, his head- and neck-feathers lightly tweaked: he shuts his eyes in happy calm, unfortunately it's most often the lower lids which slide up so that I have to infer "happy calm" from an expression of slit-eyed evil. Conversely, he nibbles gently any finger, ear, or nose presented to him. I sit on the couch reading a book; shoes off, toes moving in socks. Hip-hop, bouncing across the floor, comes Owl to nibble the toe. He is not mistaking it for food. The drabbest chunk of dog food, if he is going to eat it, draws from him at least the token pounce: a shrug of wings, a two-inch hop. He greets the toe as a friend: walks straight up to it, keeps claws on the ground, extends head with eyes shut and nibbles. What are you doing, Owl? No answer. I withdraw the foot. He follows, places a restraining claw on the toe, and nibbles. He will keep it up until it becomes a bother, so taking advantage of my greater weight I pull my foot away and put it back in the slipper. Will you tell me this, Owl, are you aware that my toe pertains to me, or do you consider my foot as a separate, independent creature which happens to follow me around a good deal? No answer.

Now, as we agreed, if it has feathers it must be a bird, and nothing which has feathers can have hair. Yet when the thick eyelids dropped over the eyes, I caught myself remarking, He's got eyelashes! "Owl," said Will, "you have bad breath." Which unfortunately is sometimes true, depending on what he last ate. Still, it is a comment you would not normally make either to your boss or to a bird. Owl spends much time at the window, his face against the pane;

when it is cool outside, the breath from his nostrils spreads two little fans of vapor on the glass.

How quiet is the flight of Owl? His "noiseless" flight, when you are watching him, is surprisingly flappy, whooshy. When occupied with other things, you are surprised to find that Owl has arrived quite nearby, maybe some time ago. For owls, that little surprise has made all the difference.

Morning. I open a kitchen cabinet: Owl. Has he been sitting in perfect darkness for ten hours, motionless, his face an inch away from the door? He is not upset.

From the window, Owl gazed skyward. His feather horns went up, he stretched up. "Ooh," he said. "*Ooh.*" Either buzzard or one of the broad-wing hawks, very high, was turning. Owl was much impressed, but did not like what he saw at all, and said softly, "Ooh."

The Saxon who first formed the word "owl" did so with skill and care, and he applied it to exactly the right bird.

Personal Habits

Owl is a *clean* bird. See him take a bath. After several minutes of scrutiny, he hops into the basin. First, he takes a drink: bends over, gets some, straightens up to let it run down his throat. Next he may plunge his head, oscillating it rapidly left-right, which sends a little spray of water to either side. Then he crouches his body almost under, vibrating wings and rump so fast that scientific-looking wave and interference patterns dimple the water, which is clouding up. As if taught by both a strict mother and the advertisements, this bird pays special attention to underwing and crotch areas: he ducks one shoulder and flaps water under the wingpit then ducks the other, and finishes with a shimmy of his tail. Slipping clumsily, he hops up and out. Wet, Owl cannot fly. Not at all, not, I am sure, if his life were to depend on it. The twenty minutes or so of flightlessness seem a fearful risk to take for a bath. Owl answers no questions about this riddle. A soaked owl looks like nothing, in the pejorative sense of the word. I do not have the heart to describe the sight further, but perhaps it is this very unappetizingness which preserves wet owls in the wild.

At this point, let's consider the pro's and con's of keeping a bird like this as a pet. First, the raptorial bird belongs in the wild, and the reasons for that judgment go on for pages. With Owl, the job was done and that was that; there was and is no good way of fitting him back into his real place. Moreover we have grown too attached to him to make the attempt.

On the positive side, Owl is not a great deal of trouble, at least not in the manner that disease-prone, delicate-stomached pets are, or those who require special environments. Indeed, your home can be his castle. On the other hand, Owl is winged appetite and as an owlet must have eaten twice as much in a day as he does now. Your hungry dog softly pleads, yearns, induces guilt; all along, however, we know old Bowzer will last until we get around to him. Hungry Owl, well, he gets on my nerves; I'll leave it at that. As a pediatrician would put it, he is on a demand schedule.

I have said that Owl is a clean bird. That is true. On the other hand, what tends to become dirty is his immediate environment. Two aspects of Owl's magnificent digestion: one, the cleanly pellets he disgorges sometime after a meal containing the proper roughage —hair, insect shells, feathers, and so forth; two, an aspect which seems, to get right down to cases, more grossly mammalian than birdlike. . . . At one point in his life, my wife, Connie, complained, "He's dumping more than he takes in." A fallacy, of course. To my almost certain knowledge, Owl does not defecate in flight, which is a good thing. Because of the mobility flight gives him, however, much is not accounted for. Somewhere . . . *somewhere* in this house, on top of a cornice or on a high bookshelf there lies heaped a fortune in guano.

When we go away for only a few days, we strip one of the bathrooms, set it up with perches and bowls of water, and leave Owl for our neighbor Wayne and his daughter Martha to take care of. We come back to a well-fed Owl and the bathroom a shambles, in the good original sense of the word. One of us scrapes and scrubs and mops the bathroom, another placates one edgy Owl who flaps from perch to person around about the house like a bird with a very short memory who has to remind himself of everything. He missed us and is resentful, is how we put it.

Otherwise, aside from his habit of shredding house-plants and of cutting into packages from the grocery which look interesting to him, Owl is a good bird.

Two Small Pleasures
Which Are Things of the Past

. . . one of which was watching daughter Lia "teach Owl to fly." She would set the fledgling on her finger, repeatedly raise and lower him. On the way down, his wings would windmill. It was easy to tease: Is that how Mother Owl does it? How can you teach without knowing how yourself?

Another was, while reading, to have Owl light on

the book or magazine. Given the chance, he would nip off corners of pages. If the book was laid flat, he would stamp down any page which tried to turn up, doing so with the peculiar vehemence which shapes many of his actions. Owl's interest in books and magazines was shallow; as soon as he realized there was nothing in them for him, he quit his investigations.

More Hex

When a person asked, "Do you just feed him birdseed like a regular bird?" it was more or less what I expected. Two or three others of good sense, however, have looked at Owl and looked at Claggart and wondered aloud which would win if a fight started. Owl's hex must have got to them as well. His talons in point of fact are longer than a cat's and the beak is designed exactly for the job, still Owl is mostly hex and feathers. "Will he bite?" we are asked. No, never. Nor scratch. A gentle bird except when being raptorial.

Sense of Humor

. . . there is agreement on it, Owl has none. He has only to run across the rug to set people laughing: in turn he mimics a hen, Groucho Marx, a little girl skipping (a hideous neckless hunchback gnome of a little girl, but like a little girl nonetheless), a man ducking rocks thrown at his head. But it is all business, he knows nor cares nothing about skipping, Groucho Marx. . . .

Before he could fly, he jumped one time to the rim of a styrofoam pseudo-straw hat; just perfectly, the hat obverted and disappeared the owlet. Laughter and applause. No, wait! Let's see what he does. But Owl "did" nothing. He sat in darkness and apathy, his patience outlasting ours.

We get a laugh, all right, in a game which he takes with unvarying seriousness. Proffer, now, a chunk of tough meat, and when he fastens his beak in it . . . don't let him take it! Owl heaves backward, flaps his wings, chitters at peak volume—if that doesn't work, he falls on his side to get his claws up. He did it as a fledgling,[*] he does it now. Come on, Owl, learn to take a joke. This all-out reaction of his is probably meant for peers, especially siblings. We note that

[*] On one crucial occasion, too immoderately: somebody's beak slipped, or the meat tore, down to the ground went the owlet. My guess.

when the claws go up—which could maim or blind a nest-mate—they grope not for the adversary but for a better hold on the meat. Owl is stubborn, not vindictive. I was about to close out this empty category, Owl's sense of humor, when two possible exceptions occurred to me. Someone taking a nap where Owl is, is likely to get his or her eyebrows yanked. That just might be Owl's idea of a joke. And then there was friend Pat, on whom Owl's joke was not. . . . Pat would bring with him his own bar in a carrying case, his idea of a joke. For retaliation, we would bring with us our own cabinet which held once a Teddy bear, another time Owl. I waited for the theatrical instant, then let them discover not a traveling bar but the traveling bird, who made the expected impression. Then he flew to my shoulder, perched two seconds, let go all down the blue sport coat. Not a bit got so far as the floor. But again, not humor unless pure ill-humor at all the foolishness.

Caution

Before man's arrival, eagle and bear and horned owl and the like had things much their own way. Now all of us are in the deepest kind of trouble, but screech owls have always had to be careful. Owl swoops on a grasshopper, his long-distance low-trajectory shot which sends him skidding across the floor on his knuckles with the insect tight-wrapped. The first thing he does, the very first thing, is to look up, and look around. What is he doing? Two things: he is looking to see in what direction his meal may be trying to escape, which is better than looking up two seconds later to wonder in which direction it *has* escaped; and since when he pounces both he and his meal attract attention, he looks up to see *if* something may be coming for him, which is better than looking up two seconds later to discover nemesis, claws first, already in midair.

Voices of Owl

"Who is making that noise, you or Owl?" which pleases me to be asked that. "What is that funny noise?" pleases me a little less; I like the noises and refer to them, to myself, as songs.

Our screech owl, *Otus asio,* does not screech.

I had collected a handful of moths from under the porch light. Flying or at least fluttering, they were to be tossed here and there for the apprentice Owl to pounce upon. As I turned to close the door, I felt a moth snatched from my fingers. Pretty slick, Owl! I took another moth, held it up, whistled. Owl kicked off from his perch and swooped it away. (People like to try this William Tell act with Owl, and it guarantees him a fair insect supply during the summer as children troop in with beetles and grasshoppers. Some, even adults, have to be reassured, and flinch a little. The hex again.) But what is the Owl's fierce cry of triumph at the kill? A soft *urk-urgle,* if he bothers to give it. The fledgling made the same sound every time he was fed: the "thank you," the parents' reward. Like the *chirrs* with which he kept in touch, the gratitude reply is about gone.

To the unpleasantnesses in his life, Owl directs a small but expressive vocabulary. The vague evils—a strange cat crossing the lawn, a bad bird gliding, shapes in the night—to them, or about them, he says, "Ooh." Food-theft he denounces by chittering. Mishandling and police brutality (e.g., touching him when he is still wet from a bath, or putting him back in the cage before he is ready) may evoke the same chittering, also beak-popping, odd little toots and grating squawks. That grating squawk is otherwise reserved for the prime hate, the sum of threat and specter and night demon, which now and then rises to disturb Owl's tranquillity. We'll get to this paradox later on.

But listen now, what sound is *that* . . . ? A woeful, anguished little cry, the sounds some small mother

33

might make if she had to watch her young being devoured by a competent but leisurely predator. What is *wrong*, Owl? Nothing is wrong. Clutched in the talons is a favorite food, the huge green katydid of summer. A few disabling nips, then, jerking his head and blinking, Owl throws it down the gullet head first and whole. Some may think that Owl's cries are cries of pity and of regret for the hierarchies of woods and meadow. The tone of the sinister remains, however, because often he addresses that cry, at much lower intensity, to whatever he is about to swoop upon. Sometimes he says nothing. Sometimes he beams a series of soft, deep trills at his target, as if to persuade it not to move. (It occurs to me, what with the variety of songs the bird has plus his inconsistency, that I have trouble keeping his lexicon straight.)

The "voice" most commonly associated with the screech owl is described by Peterson (*A Field Guide to the Birds*) as "A mournful whinny, or wail, tremulous, running down the scale. Sometimes given on a single pitch." Close enough, but to answer that call you will do better by not trying to whinny, or to wail, but to quaver a whistle while breathing out through your nose; the exhale helps with the fall in pitch and in volume.

Striving always toward system, I want to put on record that there are three main components in Owl's utterances: the whistle, the voice, and the guttural. Unfortunately, there is a whistly quality in the voice and vice versa and he mixes . . . no, he often produces a mixed . . . that is to say, there is a wide range between and . . . you will just have to listen to him. I do know this, in his second spring he broadcast a great many of those whinnies, and I am sure he was calling for another owl.

I wish I had made a note of the date. I associate it with the time his bare scaly shins—on a bird, the tarsometatarsus, not *our* shins—grew natty gray leggings for his first winter. There was enough moonlight in the dark kitchen for me to get whatever I was after without bothering to turn on the lights. All right, the scene *was* like something out of a book (specifically, this one). It *was* past midnight. I was standing at the sink and it went off right by my ear. In the shadows, I had not seen Owl perched on the rack for dish towels but there he was, his throat vibrating like a contralto's, giving out, well, just as in cartoons, in comic strips, in horror movies and comedies, and in the darkness of real woods, in slow tremolo: Whoooo. More than his throat, his whole body shook with the tremolo. That cry is taken as a bad omen in some places but I consider it a privilege to have been surprised by it right next to my ear.

We will be able to imitate that call better than we

35

can his others. Work up a fair amount of spit and keep it toward the back of your hard palate. Tilt your head back, cause the air for the whistle to bubble through the spit—it may not be the way Owl gets his tremolo but it's the best we can do. Except that it is mainly whistle, this to me is most characteristically the song of Owl. From my point of view, it is also his greeting: he gives it when we come into the empty house, when we discover him anywhere, when I come down for breakfast. Even though the song sounds diminished in bright sunlight, resonating best with darkness, Owl usually starts breakfast for me with that touch of the eerie. Erratic as my own sense of pitch is, Owl will kindly answer. And, sometimes he will not. And, sometimes he calls for no apparent reason. And, some of the apparent reasons for that song have little to do with greeting. If Owl is frightened from his perch, very likely he will turn around on the new one and aim the call back to where he was. If he lands on a "bad" perch—a newspaper I am reading, a ball, the handle of a kitchen spoon—and the thing turns or gives way under him, Owl flaps off and, as if to reassert his dignity, will trill back. In the wild, this owl song probably serves as a placing-and-spacing device and as such is anything but a greeting. When he broadcasts it, I am reminded of Gertrude Stein's little poem, "I Am Rose."

I am Rose my eyes are blue
I am Rose and who are you
I am Rose and when I sing
I am Rose like anything

And for the blue-eyed Rose we may substitute one yellow-eyed Owl.

Affable Owl, when socializing, is not noisy: a few short whoops, whistles, toots, a gritty sound, these suffice. A deeper, throatier series of toots—pigeonish—suggests a deeper affability: Owl makes them from the top shelf of a bookcase where a few small books between two much larger ones floor a would-be nest. He sounds broody. The problem of his bachelorhood will recur.

"Call Owl. We can't find him." I run through all my imitations but they never work when it counts. I try the warbled whistle which has announced almost every piece of food I have given him. No Owl. Like man's second best friend the too noble cat, he will come to the right call when he is hungry, but the point is, when Owl is in retirement he is not hungry. When he is hungry, he is all over the place. He has to be somewhere, though, and he is—half asleep in a coat closet, in a cupboard, behind a curtain. We find him the hard way and *then* he gives the low trill. But there is one way I can get his undivided attention, and I think I will say invariably. I copy the hoot of the great horned owl. Wisely, Owl does not reply. He listens, though.

Incident

Owl continues to learn about Claggart, but in the long run it may be the wrong kind of lesson. Anyway, Owl sat by the sink and worked at his chicken neck. Along came a Claggart and sprang up beside him. Owl, no Miss Muffet, crouched, glared, elbows up expanded his wings, swelling to an *enormous* owl. The cat, stiff-legged and tense as wire, tried to outface him. (While I spy from around the corner.) Owl was not outfaced. Claggart, angry between cringe and swagger, finally detoured Owl and tried to make do with scraps in the slop tray, something he would never think of doing unless he thought he could get away with it. I gave him the big yell, Claggart dropped to the floor in double shame.

Humdrum

. . . which is what Owl's life is mostly, and so have I been overemphasizing his more striking aspects? If so, I will remind that for the most part he is as everyday as a silent canary or a sleeping hamster. He is but a small bird, able to squeeze through an opening two inches by two and a quarter; tastefully attired to the point of reticence in gray check with a dull red-brown overtone, a tweedy sort and moderate in his habits; spends hours perched, doing little; will come when called only if hungry, as a general rule, otherwise scarcely answers. An orderly house with a few familiar friends, quiet, objects in their place—these things suit Owl's austere personality. Loud talk and music, jumping dancing kinds of people, too much drinking and smoking, women who move around after him in order to pat him—he perches aloof on a cornice and glares down. Most especially he dislikes strange dogs and cats, keeps between one and himself the better part of a room and all the height available. His horns up, he watches the stranger's every move, and does not approach. Having solved Jason and Claggart, he feels that that is enough dog and cat for one owl's lifetime. I say he shows good sense about that.

Parakeet

. . . you would think one bird in the house would be enough, but our youngest, Grant, wanted to give brother Will a parakeet for Christmas.

While the newcomer was being fed and watered and his cage dolled up, Owl got a good long look at the proceedings. From behind his own bars, he stared unwaveringly at the other prisoner, and he crouched forward ready to go. To dissipate that voracious longing, I gave Owl a piece of hairy beef. Impatiently he took the thing in his beak, continued his watch over the parakeet, the strip of meat dangling limp. So narrow and intense was his focus that finally the beef dropped from his beak unnoticed, like a cigarette butt from the slack lips of a thug. I told people of the encounter, keying it with Owl's membership among the raptorial birds. A most vivacious Turinese woman gave her own most characteristic interpretation: "Oh no, it was just that the owl was jealous."

As a kindness to both birds, for a while we were able to keep both cages far apart. Until convenience won out. It remains perfectly clear—contrary to the Turin insight—that Owl dearly wants a parakeet of his very own. In spite of it all, one night the two cages ended up in the same room and we even let Owl go free. A minute later I had to unknot Owl's talons from the top of the other cage. To ease the tension, I covered the parakeet's cage, top and three sides, with towels, Owl meanwhile sulking out of sight on the refrigerator. Since the open back of the cage was to the wall, I more or less assumed that from Owl's point of view the green-bird problem had been removed. Not so. Owl came back, bothered but coldly unconfused by the towels. He paced around on top of the cage, then moved toward the back. Bracing himself, leaning way over, around, and down, he glared through the uncovered bars into the dim interior, where the parakeet lacked sense to have a heart attack on the spot.

The ancients attributed to the owl great wisdom. I, more careful, attribute to him the keenest appetite to find things out. So tell me something, Owl: Were you using your Intelligence or merely your Inquisitiveness? It is all in the knowing what to look for, says Owl blandly, and makes no further answer.

Owl knows about the bars of his prison, but his longing for that bird forces him to believe that one day the parakeet's are going to give. He swoops to the side of the cage, clamps a grim array of talons around the wires, spreads his wings like Dracula's cape. Seen from over the parakeet's shoulder, Owl is death's dark angel. The parakeet, squawking, sidles over to where those hooked toes are curved around the bars, pecks at them until Owl flies away. Owl turns around to glare. Or another day while the parakeet (whose silly name I refuse to record here) fusses around with something at the bottom of his cage, Owl's hope springing eternal he tries one more time, hits the roof of the cage. He sights down between his feet. The parakeet cocks one bright idiot bead of an eye upward. Like the hero who knows he can thrash the villain because that's the way it's written in his script, slow and kind of lazy like, the parakeet uses beak over claw to hitch his way up from perch to perch until he can brace himself between his mirror and a roof bar, from which vantage point he bites the toes. Owl once more flaps off, from a safe distance tries to kill the parakeet with a hex.

Several times a week, it is the parakeet's turn to fly free. He takes salad from a spider-plant growing on a window shelf. Having nibbled a while at that, he decides next to visit his old friend Owl. He clings to the bars of Owl's cage, gibbering and peeping. (Title of the picture: "The Convict's Lawyer Comes to Visit Him after the Trial.") Owl swivels his head—he must once have heard the phrase, "shriveled him with a glance." He tries it on the parakeet, who yet again fails to shrivel, and soon Owl, full stoic, faces front, looks out at nothing.

Evolutionary Reminder

. . . in that along the shins and toes of Owl, one sees, suddenly, the scaly skin of his lizard ancestors; also their curved needle talons.

What Owl Knows

. . . it may be considerable, or perhaps he is merely adroit and is content to *appear* wise. It is hard to quiz him on the subject.

We were talking one night about such things as what the spider thinks about when it spins its web. The context was the distortion of web which occurs when the spinner has been fed experimental hallucinogenic drugs. "The spider's web," I said with a flourish, "is the spider's thought." Now and then the question of Owl's intelligence comes up, but in his case I can't be so glib. The approach to the problem lies, not through the great number of little things he has learned about our house and its inhabitants, but more through his constant zeal to find out.

Jason was asleep behind a couch: he wheezed a little, his lips flapping on the exhale. Owl was not sure about that noise. He flew to the back of the couch, glanced down to see what was there. I was rewebbing some lawn chairs: Owl lit nearby, showed more steady interest in the dismal tangle than I ever could. And likewise his interest in Connie's new hat. He is used to packages in the house, a new one draws no more than a quick look; he goes over to the window to scout a large carton in the driveway, and hoots his disapproval at it. A beebee rolls on the floor, a match is struck, a toy truck squeaks as it rolls, a piece of paper flutters to the floor: Owl attends. Yet, muttering to myself as I shuffle along, I go into a room where Owl is, and he does not even turn his head: I like to think he recognizes the footsteps.

Note that Owl has divided dogs into two categories: Jason, and all the rest. (I would like to test him with another golden retriever.) The same with cats: all except Claggart provoke the same horns-up response, and, if necessary, flight. We did test Owl with a young cat, Claggart's double, whom I call, for the best possible reason, Son-of-Harold-Claggart. Owl spooked and took off. Now almost any animal, even an invertebrate, will explore its world to some extent, and given reward or punishment in an experiment will learn appropriately to turn left or right, to distinguish relevant patterns of light or sound, each animal according to its talents, to avoid punishment and/or to seek reward. Owl, however, may approach or permit to approach two animals who have never given him any tangible reward, and moreover are the only two in his world who have ever rushed up to him close enough to scare him off. The rest, who have not really figured in his life at all, he avoids. He is not like the laboratory rat who learns that one branch of the maze will give him a shock and so keeps to the other. Well, how did this discrimination develop? We will have to be satisfied with partial answers. Whatever his feelings about Jason and Claggart, he has learned how they fit into his world. He flees the others as if it were ignorance itself he feared. What about the fact that he at least trusts any strange person? Well, we know how it is with people, they all look alike, it's hard to tell one from another. Besides, people are not very furry. It is *furry* ignorance itself which he fears. I now hint at one fearsome exception to Owl's pronouncement, one which I have mentioned before, that paradoxical haunt of the mind which, not at all furry, still excites him to a state between fright and hate. I would like to go on to say Owl chitters at the mere mention of it, but of course it is purely the thing itself. . . . It belongs to a later section.

As would be expected, Owl has learned all the perches in the house: which ones are slippery, like the banister, the washbasins, the bedposts; or may tilt or swing, like the large wicker breadbasket, the wooden salad spoon; which ones he can hit at a thousand miles an hour, like the neck of the standing gooseneck lamp and the arm of the sofa. Will's parakeet learned some of the same things but in doing so spent much of its time in panicky whirring about—hitting glass, getting stuck behind a bookcase or under the washing machine. What was remarkable about Owl, during the short period it took for him to complete his exploration of the house, was the purposive way he went about it. He would take readings on each prospective perch, his head swinging like a bob on a rubber band. Try it out, back to the original one, on to a familiar one, then to the new one again. These short, careful flights crisscrossed the house for no apparent purpose except to get it all mapped, not just by eye but also by wing and by foot. (The very last perch to be mapped was the pipe in the shower stall. Summer nights, when all doors are open, he flies up there in secret. His morning songs have wakened us more than once. I see him watching us over the top of the glass door. As I have discovered myself, there are at least two pitches which resonate and/or echo off the tiles, and Owl has found one of them.)

It is oddly pleasant to be there when Owl flies up the stairs, or glides down them.

Owl keeps track of things, sometimes better than I do. I give him a chicken neck and before long it is gone, I forget about it. Some days later, Owl brings out what looks like a finger bitten from a mummy. It would seem to be of purely archeological interest, but there he is, hooking into it, twisting, tugging. For all I know, it may date not from three days before but three months before. He keeps them where it is hard

to reach. Do you hoard them, Owl, or do you simply drop them when you are full and discover them later by accident? No answer. I will answer for him: he hoards. Many rodents do so, no great wisdom is required; people hoard as well, we can call it neither vice nor virtue without knowing the circumstances.

Glass has posed a special kind of test for Owl. He has learned about it, but he doesn't quite believe in it. Before he could really fly, he discovered the second hand of the stove clock and made one good try for it. He had to give up on it, of course, but not until he had made a few cautious, half-hearted little strikes from close up. Later, when full flight expanded his domain, he came across other electric clocks. Each second hand in turn drew that same pessimistic I-know-it's-no-use-but-anyway sort of pounce, and the same for the swinging pendulum inside a glass-cased clock: he seemed to know the setup wasn't honest but he had to try. His first encounter with the tropical fish in my aquarium was a different matter. He hit the glass with full enthusiasm—once. Now, he watches them from a nearby bookshelf with the absorption of a true hobbyist. Knowing the difference between himself and an osprey, he has never tried to swoop on a fish from the top.

For a few days we kept a little brown snake (*Storeria*

dekayi) in a jar.* Owl wanted that snake, and badly. Unable to make it through the narrow mouth of the jar, he dropped down to the table top. He bowed, gave the snake the big glare, swung his head, and then, which set the children to applauding, did a wonderful little dance of vexation all around the jar. The snake meanwhile was wriggling around in the patch of grass in the bottom. It was too much to be borne, Owl hopped at the snake and was not convinced until he had tried from several angles. It was easy to read fury into his movements and expression.

Owl would be a good bird to put to an intelligence test—which is not to say that necessarily he would achieve a high score on it. But, as we have seen, he is all too easily motivated to try; he has a very decisive way of entering into situations, and one thing that bird does is pay attention. Teachers, parents, experimentalists will appreciate those qualities. As soon as time and ingenuity permit, I intend to set up some simple problem with which to challenge Owl. Now, for lack of relevant tests and scales, and for fear of falsifying up or down, I am not going to attempt any firm comparative estimate of Owl's intelligence. Instead,

---

* A number of snakes get brought to the house for identification. Each usually arrives tagged as a baby rattler or copperhead; and invariably—so far —leaves with a name something like Milquetoast's lesser worm-snake, *Innocua nondescripta.*

let us continue to observe him as he goes on about his business—fly, spy, exclaim, poke and pry, pick up and discard, watch, examine, stalk, strike, work and play— and be satisfied with this broad evaluation: an active and inquiring mind, if not a great one; original and interesting, though short of true creativeness; practical rather than idealistic; pragmatic rather than insightful; at times mysterious in its workings, yet lacking the depth of mysticism; more retentive than systematic; a mind responsive to, perhaps even dominated by, the senses; yet, above all respectful and acquisitive toward knowledge.

Health-Food Fanatic

. . . Owl is not one. Still, we had a Christmas cactus all budded out and ready to be gift-wrapped, only Owl got to it first and nipped off each little bud and ate it. Ever since the time he tore the cellophane from a head of lettuce and had himself a quick simple salad, that as a very young bird, we have seen to it that he gets his fruit and greens. I don't know whether he needs them or not, but he partakes with dainty messiness . . . berries yes, lemon and grapefruit no, orange yes with much beak-smacking somewhat like you or me with a lemon slice, beans carrots potatoes no,* onion no, any leafy green yes. Yes in that he picks the greenery to pieces some few of which he swallows. Owl was perched on a glass of water, I gave him a piece of spinach. He dipped it in the water, shredded some off, dipped the remainder again . . . on and on. You can watch an obsession like that only so long, it begins to get on your nerves. When I returned, Owl was off somewhere, having left around the glass forty-five (that's ten plus ten plus ten plus ten plus five) spinach particles and about ten more in the water. (This grim counting business reminds me of the time an ominous herd of buzzards seemed to fill half the sky over our neighborhood. Knowing a close count would be more impressive than any guess of "millions and millions," I ticked off squads of five while the buzzards milled obligingly around and around and drew in additions from all horizons. I counted, re-counted, made another estimate when finally they all headed off southeast. By the time I found somebody to tell about it, I had forgotten the number. There sure were a lot of them though.) Why does Owl *do* these things? Since I can't get a reasonable answer, I suggest he doesn't know why himself, perhaps he is losing his mind.

* He will swallow *one* of almost anything put directly to his beak; the question is whether, once he takes something out of his mouth with his claws, he puts it back in again or drops it.

A Screech Owl Is Not a Lap Dog

. . . ours, nevertheless, does not conform to the image of the lonely hunter in his forest who has just two questions for anything that moves: Can I catch and eat it? Or can it catch me? Owl, as we have seen, likes to be tweaked and groomed, especially around the head and neck. Pull away before he has had enough and a claw flicks out to retrieve the finger. (You're a nice bird, Owl.) As one works affectionately around the back of the head and toward the front again, one arrives at a small patch of dark feathers diagonally under the bill which immediately triggers him to respond in kind. He nibbles back. (See parentheses preceding.) This kind of activity—consider also his spontaneous pulling of ear lobes, hair, eyebrows—may be simply a confused extension of what goes on between parent and offspring and between courting owls in coldest springtime; still and all he's pretty good company.*

---

*When my soul is at its most disturbed, I sometimes wonder: Suppose while Owl nibbles a finger or ear lobe—mine, anyone's—a raw chunk thereof were to strip off . . . and Owl had unlimited appetite . . . and the person unconscious . . . would Owl keep eating until the person was all gone? I keep this macabre thought down where it belongs, in a footnote.

At Table with Owl

. . . for a while a delightful novelty while he oversaw us from the chandelier or strode stiffly about among the supper things; or, to show manners more precise than anyone's, balanced on the rim of a water glass and sipped (which divides the world into three classes, those who send back to the kitchen for another glass, those who surreptitiously wipe the rim, and those who get right on with it).

Connie's mother's bridge partner was with us for breakfast, as was Owl overhead on a cornice. The late-morning Sunday sun seemed to slant in from two sides at once and in particular lit up our guest's plate. As I came back in from the kitchen with the coffeepot, I noticed Owl beginning to lean forward into that diver's crouch of his, and I sat down with a sense of foreboding. Between eggs and sausage, our guest's wedge of tomato was gleaming like . . . like . . . well, whatever simile I was going to use doesn't matter, what did matter was Owl's: Like *meat!* To sit, as the talk goes on, and to know a piece of the immediate future that no one else knows (or at most one other) (who does not know you know) is to share for a moment the prophet's power and woe. I suppose at the last second for effect I might have stretched my arm out to designate the tomato marked for destruction but I didn't think of it. Anyway, Owl came down somewhere over my left shoulder and made his kill. Noise, laughter, commotion. Owl glanced up and around, businesslike, very stern in the midst of all the hullabaloo. Record here Mrs. Tenney's name on the all-time list of good sports. Owl was not enthusiastic about tomato, he was given a few mouthfuls of egg instead.

Owl has been receiving few if any further invitations to dine with us. The novelty has given way to irritation. Owl's bowels move best around mealtime. And who wants a wild-eyed barbarian dinner guest who with beak, claw, and nasty noise disputes every forkful with you? While howling children take his side in the contest and offer him consolation prizes any time he loses.

Tufts

. . . they're there, we presume they serve a purpose. Why is it that when Owl sees something disturbing or suspicious his horns go up? Because he thinks that with such tufty ears and gleaming eyes and ferocious claws he looks like a lynx. He believes it, we won't argue.

Sunbaths

What's this nocturnal bird of prey doing sunning himself? It seems out of character. A bright patch of sunlight on the kitchen floor. Owl checks right, left, locates the dozing Claggart, then softly flies down to it—there is something special about these quiet landings, he sifts the air through feathers as he lets himself down. (Other times he seems to hit the perch as hard as he can. The gooseneck standing lamp he enjoys making go *klong* against the wall.) Owl centers himself in the light, looks around once more, and gradually extends, expands wings and tail feathers like fans out on the floor—a fine, brightly-illuminated gray-brown display of Owl all spread out there, with watchful yellow eyes. . . . Now Claggart is up, and walking toward Owl, who, of late, no longer takes off. Claggart is tangled wire pulled tight, as he gets near his walk becomes crabby and slow. Owl's head rotates to the cat's progress but he does not gather himself up in the least, will not interrupt his sunbath. The hard glare keeps the cat to a careful detour around Owl, even though he is close enough for an easy pounce. I don't know what game it is they're playing. I remind you of Claggart's pugnacity, which has been inscribed on the skins of X number of dogs and 10 X number of other tomcats. (Also some few people, although the cause is not pugnacity. For the woman who grieves, "Why did he bite—scratch—me?" the proper reply runs as follows: "I am afraid your touch has over-excited him. You can calm him down by rubbing him under the chin." It happens to be the truth.)

Owl may also fly to a lampshade and stretch himself out over the flow of light and warm air up from the bulb. The light glows through every feather. He is a splendid lampshade himself.

His sunbaths are odd, unowlish, but appealing. What I don't like is to see him go down to Jason's bowl and peck dog food out of it like some sidewalk pigeon.

Heart's Abhorrence

That unpleasant grating squawk is coming forth from Owl. We turn to see what's wrong, and find what is now one nasty-looking little bird. He has elongated himself up to what must be twice his usual stature (which still doesn't come to any imposing much) at half his usual thickness. What shows most is a wide-open beak and a lot of pink mouth and tongue, where the noise keeps coming from. His horns poke way up. His eyes are all yellow around dots of pupil. For God's sake, Owl, what is it . . . ? There is no longer any mystery about what it is that sets him off to such a peak of bad feeling, the question is *why*. You may be somewhat disappointed in the class and range of objects he so detests: broom or mop or axhandle, wooden rifle, baseball bat, fireplace poker, stick, long knife . . . anything at all like those. The object must be made to move and be somewhere near the vertical. If you hold the whatever-it-is at the horizontal, you may be able to sneak it by him without provoking an outburst; but once he has raged at it, he is not fooled, not soothed by your putting it level again.

There is something not quite rational about Owl. I might even call him irrational. Even anti-rational.

I deny that Owl, deserve it or not, has ever been thrashed with a stick, broom handle, anything. Nor has anyone ever struck him in any way. No surprise then that he sits unperturbed when I come at him with arm upraised, fist clenched. But if I bring a piece of kindling wood up to him, he shows his hate right to the last instant. Usually, inside a one-foot limit, he will fly away; several times he has dared to give the thing a sudden bite. In generalizing about Owl's habits, I keep having to use "often," "usually," "perhaps," "probably." On this topic, I use the word "always." I've never known him to fail. There is a mechanical, stereotyped mindlessness in the way he will repeat the response over and over: up goes the stick, up go the horns, and *grrich!* I can calm him by patting his head, stroking the excited tufts down again. Then raise the stick, up go the horns again. A determined experimentalist would have found out by now how many times in rapid succession Owl will react. I have tried five or six presentations but quit after that because he gets so unpleasant about it, and we have no spare owls should this one give out.

Well now. Here we have a package of behavior, not learned, resistant to change, dependable as a light-switch, and with the same sort of inflexibility.* The only noteworthy variation depends on how The Thing comes at him: at his level or below, and Owl stretches up as if trying to face The Thing down; from above, and Owl argues from a crouch. Like nest-building in many birds, the reaction seems to have been written directly into the genes. (I am assuming our Owl "equals" all screech owls.) And what a creature is born with tends to be important to the species—it may be disastrous, there is no guarantee that any behavior

* In behavioristic psychology the term for this sort of reaction was "unconditioned reflex"; and probably still is.

57

pattern will promote the interests of a group throughout the course of evolution, just the same "innate" strongly indicates "important." Consider also the nature of his reaction. "Real" threats such as a strange dog or cat coming up to him, these he simply escapes, saving any display of disapproval until he gets to a safer place. Shape in the night, bad bird in the sky, big carton in the driveway, such things he hoots quietly at, as if to warn others. He *grates* at adversity—mishandling, food-theft—while the erect tufts indicate a degree of fear or at least of excitement; the gaping beak is reserved for the appearance of The Thing. (I would think of an exception. The first time Owl went by car, the chaotic stream of world around the windows terrified him and he put on his fear-hate display. He must have thought the world had all come unglued. Lia at two and a half climbed into a train just like any other building until, from a perfectly smooth start, the world began to ooze by. She was about as scared as Owl, but recovered more quickly.) I would like to ask Owl what it is that's shaped like a stick, moves, and exacerbates screech owls—knowing that since he has no sense of humor we will get a straight answer. But since he has never lived in the forest where he might encounter the prototype of what we're discussing, he does not have the answer.

So it's up to us. The first thing to come to mind is

snake. But Owl has been presented with a small live one, larger freshly killed ones, a tube made to wriggle in a most snake-like fashion, and a lifelike plastic imitation. Owl coldly measures each for size, and if it's small enough he goes for it. If larger ones are advanced on him, he simply takes off. I think of unlikely things—firearms, even the Indian's bow and arrow, but nothing makes any sense. Weasel perked upright? Squirrel? There is little point in a screech owl's standing its ground, considered from the viewpoint of species or individual survival, unless it means to defend the nest. What looks like a stick and robs nests? I give up. I now transfer the subject from natural science to religion. Dr. Sam, our esteemed neighbor, is a minister. On his next visit, I intend to provoke Owl with a crucifix. Owl will rage against it like the Devil's nephew. That, or like an innocent soul possessed of the Devil. In either case, Sam can make the decision and deal with the problem on theological grounds.

Blood

On vacation, we took Owl with us to the Red Cottage. Five hundred miles in a compact car with Connie Lia Will Grant Jason Claggart & Owl.

And luggage for three weeks. I can say that Owl travels well, once we learned the necessity of screening the scenery from him. A large old barn of a place with unfinished inside walls, its ceilings way up out of reach, the Cottage is ideal for an Owl. The many high beam ends, open sills, and deep recesses become his forest. Crickets abound; katydids, prodigious moths wing in from the woods and meadows of all Connecticut to crowd around the lightbulbs. There are many visitors and guests, also fifteen to twenty cousins in varying ages and kinships: Owl entertains them all with his tameness, his strutting, posturing, his bug-snatching. All day and much of the night the doors swing open and shut, now and then an unscreened window is opened, and so the thought recurs, Someday Owl may leave. And the next thought is, The boy should learn to hunt . . . to catch mice. And any time the uproar ceased in the Red Cottage, one could hear them: behind canisters along kitchen shelves, in closets, inside interior walls, under cupboards and the refrigerator, inside interior walls: mice.

The green plant—algae or grass or tree—grows in the sun; the animal at the bottom of the order—protozoan or grasshopper or moose—feeds on that green; and riding upon that herd, regulating it, the predators of the world—amoeba, robin, tiger . . . before, sooner or later, gradually or suddenly, the parasites and scavengers and final fungi and bacteria return us to something for the plants. The quick cruel interest is in the hunter. I wanted to see what Owl could do.

One afternoon a mouse, dazed and probably sick, presented itself in the driveway. While I stalked it from the rear, brother-in-law Fred made such noises and movements as were cunningly calculated to distract and confuse the mouse without scaring him into flight. (Fred is a lawyer.) I clapped the lid of a trashcan over the mouse. ("*Now* what do we do?") We managed to catch the mouse directly, and, after waiting a number of hours to let Owl work some of his last meal through his system, we delivered it to him: Owl was set on a high shelf in the bathroom and the mouse was committed to the tub, which I had lined with an old curtain.

Except when full and sleepy, at which times his eyes go half-shut in Oriental meditations, Owl has no casual glance. His most everyday turn of the head delivers what I am entitled to call a piercing glare. What he gave that first mouse he had ever seen, if photographed, might be hard to tell apart from a photo of his looking at an ant he has no intention of bothering with. Nevertheless and more than ever, he immediately became Owl to the utmost, all eyes, and beak, and knuckles tight around the edge of the shelf as he crouched and leaned. The mouse meanwhile poked around on the canvas in the bottom of the bathtub, paying no attention to the eyes on him nor to the juvenile feeding *chirrs* Owl was beaming at it. And nothing happened. Minutes went by. We shifted from foot to foot, exchanged some tense jokes: "If looks could kill . . ." "That's why his mother threw him out of the nest—he wouldn't eat mice." Disparaging remarks were made, I defensively pointed out that, after all, Owl had been fed just that morning. Minutes went by. Owl never *has* liked a lot of spectators standing around. Tension gave way to boredom, and I decided to put Owl on a fast for half a day or so: thin him down while we fattened the mouse up. But then at last and finally, Owl made his little diver's hop off the edge and dropped softly on the mouse. With the mouse in his clutch, Owl as always looked up to check right, left, front, back.

I had brought with me a small knife with which to dispatch the mouse in case Owl was slow about it. Later I was to discover that Owl, while indifferent, happens to execute fairly quickly. At the time, he seemed to us agonizingly slow and inefficient: he would give a random nibble here and there, glance up —that every few seconds—then perhaps tug briefly at a leg or the tail. We only wondered that the mouse made no sign of resistance. And I did not use the knife, for reasons which contribute to whatever it is which supports boxing matches, bullfights, cockfights, hunting to hounds, war, screen carnage, trapped-bird shoots. Obvious at last that the mouse was dead. We watched, puzzled, for perhaps ten minutes; came back after another ten and saw no change in the situation: Owl still at work, glancing up every few seconds in what looked like nervous irritation. The mouse might as well have been made of vinyl. In the next five or ten minutes to himself, however, he took the head off and ate it—that, as I have read and seen, the *Strigidian* custom—after which I saw him reduce the body by three or four twisting tugs and then swallow the rest at a gulp. Owl lifted himself up through the air to the shelf over the bathroom door.

The blooded Owl. A mouse, compared in evolution to Owl, mouse virtually my next-of-kin, Owl little else than a hot-blooded feathered flying lizard, whose very feathers indeed evolved from the lizard's scales. I had traduced the mammal into the claws of the lizard's cousin . . . not genuine misgivings, those, merely academic reflections.

Fred went to the hardware store and picked up for us a trap which catches mice unharmed, in anticipation of which a hundred some years ago Schopenhauer wrote: "The pleasure in this world, it has been said, outweighs the pain; or, at any rate, there is an even balance between the two. If the reader wishes to see shortly whether this statement is true, let him compare the respective feelings of two animals, one of which is engaged in eating the other.''

Mice came to the trap. I became an indoor, humble kin to the falconer. The second mouse was struck as soon as seen, and killed with one thrust of the hooked beak through the eye socket into the brain. Forgetting that Owl sees very little up close, I assumed he had learned to execute with this one decisive stroke. Again, Owl nibbled until I went away and during my absence ate the head. It is a strange ritual; all or most owls seem to insist on it. I have wondered and asked about it. I thought I had some sort of clue in the following paradox. Given an unusually big mouse, Owl is unable, or at least very unwilling, to take off with it, but when he has that same weight inside him, he can of course fly perfectly well. And, once he has swallowed the head, he is able and likely to fly off with the body and take it to a more secure place. Owl is not simply arranging his ballast, however. Even the largest owls, who can fly away with almost anything they kill, are reported to eat the heads first, and if food is plentiful they will eat the heads in preference to the rest . . . despite the teeth and all that bone.

It is a harsh supervision which the raptors keep over rodent numbers and, indirectly, over rodent health. We saw how the first mouse, so incompetent that even

Fred and I could catch it, was finally taken as inert as a chunk of beef. The second, though healthy and active, was not alert to what was coming down on him. The third was a different brand of rodent. Trapped in the kitchen, imprisoned overnight with the heartiest of last meals, it was put into the arena in the morning. Owl, hungrier than usual, swooped instantly to clutch only cloth. The mouse had jumped out of the way and easily kept that one jump ahead of Owl. For ten seconds, less, the two of them bounced around inside the bathtub before Owl lifted on out and up to his shelf, there to take aim again. Another strike, another nothing, this time Owl did not stay in the tub to try to mix it with the mouse: there must be a written-in warning to small owls that to scrimmage around on the forest floor is to invite trouble. Owl, re-perched, stared down at this veritable Douglas Fairbanks of a mouse, and stayed put. The mouse reached into ever new resources. Exploring the arena for escape, he came to the chain of the plug with which I had stoppered the too-obvious mouse-hole. Up, up that chain! One great leap! Away! And straight line down a real mouse-hole in the wood floor. He did not pause; but I have him doing so at the rim of the tub between the hot and cold handles to wave his plumed hat at us in farewell. Farewell, Douglas Fairbanks!

All subsequent mice get caught. I take to letting

them go on the kitchen floor: the path of each converges with Owl's—lines made to cross by fate. Owls and mice are the closest of associates. I learn that while this small owl does not have very much cutting power in his beak, he kills in less than a minute, sometimes less than thirty seconds. After the first few "random nibbles," Owl sometimes becomes nonchalant and we see him look up holding his meal by only a hind leg: the mouse is already dying or dead. (The apparent nonchalance is misleading. When eating common food, Owl is irritable enough. With a mouse, the least touch or even an approach . . . "berserk" is what comes to mind but it's far too strong a word. "Hostile" is about right.)

To cut down the number of mice using the Red Cottage, we tried for a while ordinary spring traps. I found a mouse half alive, half dead in one, as it must have been for hours. I ended the mouse, we stopped using the spring traps, I delivered the body, with a long thread tied to its leg, to Owl. The idea at first was to simulate a moving, dodging target, but Owl had the thing immediately. All right—I would simulate prey vigorously resisting. The meal, wrapped entirely in claws, still hopped and slid along the floor. Owl was as baffled as you would be by a beefsteak's suddenly flexing, bucking, medium-rare. Yet his bafflement held an accidental shrewdness, and in it Owl told something about himself. It did not occur to him to fight to subdue the mouse. With paranoid accuracy, he glared everywhere around him for the source of the trouble, and let out his grating creaks of protest—the ones he makes when an alien disturbs him at mealtime. Apparently it is written: A struck mouse is a dead mouse. And no jumping corpse can tell him different.

Do you believe in voodoo? Nor do I, and it is a good thing neither does my wife's aunt. She had kindly given us combings of silver hair to give to Owl with his meat. After one of these meals, Owl took a mouse. The next day, he coughed up his pellet, the skull and tiny bones, all tightly wound and bound in Aunt Caddy's silver hair.

We continue to struggle to make sense out of the capricious Owl's behavior. Finding Owl slow to take a certain mouse, I put the bird on a fast while the mouse feasted. The fast, for one reason or another, lasted not the intended day but almost two, so when finally I let the mouse go I quickly stepped back out of the way so as not to be struck down by the feathered fury. Who drew himself stiffly up, poked ear tufts up, regarded the mouse as if something entirely new and a little frightening. The mouse crossed the floor and began to follow the wall, an easy meal at any point. Owl made short flights and hops along the terrain of chair backs and table tops above the mouse, tracking it but always in a posture of curiosity and unease. The mouse (a nonresident) crossed another open space, which should have been a fatal mistake, but still Owl sat tight. It was not until the mouse had made its way to what should have been safety, the junk corner— where were stacked boots, bicycle pump, three-legged music stand, coil of rope, hatchet, as well as a great number of Thing-like objects—that Owl made his swoop. He had to make his catch directly under the tripod, gave himself a fair thump against the wall in doing so, and ended up with wings hung up on this and that. Which is doing it the hard way, Owl. It was one of your small mysteries, like why you shred greens into confetti or why you nip the corners from pages; not one of the great ones, like why you insist on beheading the mouse or why you hate the sight of a moving upright stick.

Another small mystery. Regard the mounted deer's head* which wears a cane-cutter's wide-brimmed straw hat, an old American flag in its antlers, and holds a cigarette in its mouth. The immediate mystery is not which visitor to the Red Cottage set up this display, or why, but why Owl repeatedly sails full force into that thatch of straw as if he wanted someone

---

* Owl might well wonder why human beings would want to leave the choice part, the head, up on the wall to spoil while they use only the leftover torso.

to exclaim, "Man, he hit that hat like a hundred-pound eagle!" When he poses right alongside the flag we can say, "Plainly, he thinks he's the national bird." But why does he keep after that old grass hat? I think enough has been said about Owl for you to make your own guess.

"Oh Owl you are *cute!*" "You are the funniest thing I ever saw." "Can I touch him? Can I hold him?" "Let me feed him something." Ones like what Owl and I judge to be genuine compliments; we discount those that are addressed to me in the form of, "That certainly must be an interesting pet. Doesn't he make, ah, messes?" If Owl put up a pink ribbon for every one of the spontaneous outbursts addressed to him, his cage would be as decked with frills as some perverse boudoir. For each ribbon, however, or compliment, he would far rather have one live mouse.

Prisoners, Captives, Pets

. . . an example of each, in that order, would be the monkey in the pet store; the hamster or guppy family in the home; your dog or your cat. Which category for Owl? You would not like to see a swallow kept in the house, or even a cardinal. What about keeping an owl as a cage bird? And since he does spend half the day or more behind bars, we might as well call him that. We wonder whether our bird wants out. Often, right after a big meal, he will take to the window sill and watch whatever may be going on outside, and it is plain he can't be scouting for more food. The question is open. If Owl has a preference, he usually makes it known. When he wants out of his cage, it sounds from the next room as if "the poor thing is battering itself to death." Take a peek in: Owl is deliberately working on the bars with his claws and hopping back and forth from perch to coffee can (his home within a home within a home) making the can roll and clank. He may not be bruising himself in wild yearning for the skies—something like that—but he gives the impression of too much energy to be contained so narrowly. Other times, motionless, he faces out through the bars like a political prisoner who is waiting for his conspirators to overthrow the government and put the jailers to death. Sometimes he seems to feel not confined *enough,* and he backs into the coffee can, a container filled with tweedy feathers and set with yellow eyes, then these close and it's nothing but feathers. If he has eaten enough or too much, or dislikes the company in the room, he refuses to leave his cage unless coaxed; maybe not even then. Or, for reasons known only to himself, he will not voluntarily go back into it, but must be nudged, poked, hustled under vocal protest—the way the police urge a drunk-and-disorderly into the cage who happens to be of some standing in the community. The next time, as I hold the door open for him, he may bounce in from a foot away. I conclude then, that since Owl has clear ways of expressing his displeasure, but rarely does so, that he is reasonably content.

Which is not the whole issue. Hawk, great cat, ape, raccoon—none of them spends much time howling or shaking the bars for freedom. Each, in a sense, is content. But who likes to see them in that kind of contentment? Each has its own range of habits, adaptations, capabilities, whatever, and when there is no arena for these to be acted out the prisoner becomes a stuffed animal which happens still to be eating and drinking. The hawk may not feel the lack—or it may—of open sky from which to strike down at its prey yet the visitor to the aviary should; and also feel the lack of earth in the cage of guinea pigs—that third or fourth dullest captive—for the beasts to dig their community burrows into.

Now back to Owl. His folk do not soar like eagles, take intercontinental flights like geese, nor wing around like swifts. It would be a pleasure to watch a flock of migratory owls drift through a forest, but such is not their way. Nonetheless, fly is what they do. The longest possible flight in our house—from, say, the southwest corner of the kitchen around and up to his perch on some guano-streaked books in my study upstairs—is pretty short, yet he generally breaks even this excursion into shorter legs. He prefers to fly to a spot he can see from where he sits. I decide that while Owl's range is cramped, what he does around the house is not entirely different from what he would do free. He swoops on his prey, he socializes (this probably far more than normal), prowls, bathes, pries into things. But in March, Owl calls and calls. We tend to keep the same hours, he and I, but in March in the dull morning gray of six o'clock his rattling cage keeps a person awake. We open the windows, weather permitting, to see if maybe he can call someone in. No answer from the woods. Under these circumstances, the vigils Owl keeps at the window take on poignancy.

Bachelorhood

The question, not until now written out, arises at last: How do we know Owl is a *he?* We don't. Young Will asserts he has read somewhere that male screech owls are darker, and ours certainly is darker than most of the pictures I have seen, but no source of mine backs up Will's claim. We continue to plan for Owl's nuptial, we continue to search. At the Red Cottage in midsummer, against all likelihood, Connie discovered another *Otus asio,* not in the meadows, not in the hemlock forest, but at the hairdresser's. There was a fifty-fifty chance that the sexes were right but the season was wrong, and both owls too young. . . . We did not introduce them.

Like any other mortal, Owl cannot ignore a mirror. The ones he is familiar with draw only a passing glare. A new one, or a reflection seen from some fresh perspective—he bobs, crouches, and looks and looks and looks. Toward the end of his second spring, Connie tested or teased or tormented Owl with a new mirror, the one in the lid of her curler-box. He showed the sharpest curiosity, then let's say pretended to lose interest, and went off. She set the box to one side. Owl, possibly carrying the lingering memory of someone lovely inside the lid of that box, came winging in on it, knocked everything to the floor.

On the lawn of an old house surrounded by high oaks, I heard one night the breathy trill of a whistle which curved down and out. I made, unembarrassed, the best answers I could. The whistles went on, probably independent of my own. (It is a foible of the bird-watcher that when he spaces his imitations among the bird's calls, the bird is then answering him.

He is more likely answering the bird, who sings on oblivious to his noise.) I ran through my owl vocabulary, might just as well have been trying to wheedle the oak trees.

A visit to the Children's Museum, where a quick glimpse of caged eyes and beak fooled me a moment: a fledgling horned owl, very much the wrong type. A big downy blur of an owl, slow in its movements, almost dreamy. I was told it eats only killed meat, still refuses anything alive. Its neighbor is a parrot, and when the fledgling is hungry it turns to the parrot, clings to the partitions, and begs. The parrot is unmoved. Eyes and fluff . . . I looked at the outsize talons—true meathooks—the one indicator of what the owl's career could be; and recalled infant Hercules in some illustration, born all baby except for hands already strong enough to strangle the serpent which was destined to crawl into his crib.

We persist. I heard from nearby woods the familiar whistle. I made a few counterfeit replies, then rushed inside to get Owl, who was perched at the window. He was not whistling, or whinnying, in return, but was giving out the little *woo-ooh* which I have associated, and I guess he does too, with fear or high curiosity. I caged him and set the cage on top of a car. Owl kept up his small noises. Except for insects and treefrogs, dogs, cars, an occasional airplane, the night was . . . I was going to say quiet, but as a matter of fact it was pretty noisy out there. Then some kind of hoot owl broadcast. In contrast to the five-note cathedral tones of the great horned owl, this one was sounding off a dashing mix of long and short phrases. Barred owl, perhaps. All smaller owls went off the air.

A recent encounter reminds me of an event in Gavin Maxwell's *Ring of Bright Water:* after the killing of his marsh otter, Maxwell searched and searched for a replacement without success—*Lutrogale perspicillata maxwelli* being after all a most exotic beast—until one day from the door of his hotel he saw to his astonishment a related and equally exotic specimen being led by on a leash like any spaniel. It was as if the force of his wish had caused the animal to materialize some thousands of miles from its habitat. Anyway, behind our house stands an old cranky-looking Spanish oak. Twenty-five branchless feet up, there is a hole in the trunk, about rat-size, in good view from our bedroom window. This cavity worries, aggravates me. First, it indicates the tree may be rotten in the heartwood, in which case some southeast blast may bring it down like a hammer of judgment on our frame house. Second, we need and want that tree right where it is, therefore if it is reasonably sound the cavity should be cleaned out, screened, and set with a pipe drain at the bottom. Which costs, though less than to have it cut down. And that less than having it extracted from the middle of our house. Third, no bird or other animal seems ever to take advantage of that homey-looking cavity. . . . I was outside dumping the garbage, or some such high endeavor, and saw in the weak light from the outside lamp a gray-white entity clinging to the rough bark not six feet up, in fact just where some winters ago I had driven a big nail to attach suet. Behind me in the kitchen Owl was whistling and whinnying. I added some encouraging sounds, just trying to sound like one of the owl-gang, the small whistle notes Owl makes when calm but busy at something. "Connie," I said over my shoulder, "there's a *screech owl* out here. Get the flashlight." During the quarrel over the whereabouts of the flashlight, the visitor hiked around to the other side of the tree. Since owls by reputation are not timid, I openly circled the tree with the flashlight scanning trunk and branches. It took a while to spot the visitor, when I did I found we had lost a mate for Owl but gained of all things a flying squirrel. Whom I now officially welcome.

About his second otter, Maxwell wrote: ". . . the meeting of the only man in the British Isles who was trying desperately to find a home for a pet otter with the only man who was searching, with equal desperation, for an otter." Well, coincidences like that do happen. At this very moment, it may be that someone is writing an ad for our local newspaper, a peculiar ad about an *Otus asio,* and is ending it, "Object: Matrimony."

Experiments with Eyes

If, as I suggested earlier, you set your own screech owl on your hand, get his or her attention fixed on your face, or on some other object of more than fleeting interest, and then slowly move your hand around about through short distances, you will notice something odd. The owl's head remains almost perfectly stationary while the body gyrates under the very flexible neck. The owl switches the case with the familiar Hindu dancer—the sidewinding head—and goes the dancer many dimensions better: right left up down front back around about pivot and tilt, in any combination. It would take several sets of gyroscopes, don't ask me how many, to duplicate this stability in space, though obviously Owl is using his eyes, not his balance organs. When his sight is not riveted to a spot in particular, Owl does not play the game. It's as cute as all get-out, but why does he do it? By way of an oblique answer, imagine Owl on a swaying twig in a tree, moonlight and high wind, as he takes aim on a creeping mouse. His body vacillates while his head stays still. All right. If he *needs* a fixed point from which to aim, he is admitting to a rigid type of tracking system. It is a little as though he had to aim his swoop the way you would aim a rifle, and "fire" himself like its bullet. Perhaps he does not enjoy the same "big picture" the adult human eye obtains, does not have quite the visual mastery of his world. But if that fixed line of sight, the stable platform for the eyes, are necessary, why the head-swing and bob before taking off? Wouldn't he get the same benefit from swaying around on his branch? No, when he bobs and swings his head, the muscle-nerve circuits tell him just how much this way and that he has displaced his head, and he compares this displacement with how much things move in relation to each other out there. Then he knows what's what. Or what's where. When the twig is tossing every which way in the wind, he is not producing the movements and so can't make any comparisons. It all seems pretty complicated. The mouse should escape before he has worked it all out. But even though Owl missed Douglas Fairbanks, and that one several times, he can still point with pride to the rest of his record: no misses.

And I recall now . . . while Owl swings his head a moment before swooping, in the last seconds before he goes, his stare is fixed and fatal. It is hard to gain a clear idea of the strengths and limitations of Owl's see-and-strike system. He markedly prefers an unmoving target. Unless very hungry, he will watch and watch some erratic prey, grasshopper or mouse, as it moves about; and then the prey will stop and, uncannily, seem to wait for Owl to descend on it. While bragging about how exceedingly rare are his misses, he forgets that his prey is dislocated and set loose in Owl's own territory. Having had to chase them down myself, I can tell you that even something like a grasshopper is easier to catch on the kitchen floor than it is in tall grass. On the other hand, Owl might remind us that he can pick a moth out of the air. I've seen you do it once, Owl, just exactly once. You are no flying ace. If it were urgent, presumably, he could sharpen the talent. Suppose that while Owl is in flight his target does move. He can adjust, I've seen him do it, but his ability is limited: running away is futile but a quick last-second hop may be effective. (As for evasive tactics, incidentally, it really does help to be one of a scattering flock—if we can use a single anecdote. Owl went for a moth which happened to have landed among some paper patches a child had cut out. The downdraft stirred them up, though not the moth. Owl came down flat-footed in their midst. I would say he looked foolish but he put on the same old expression of acute ferocity.)

79

With him perched on my hand, zeroed in on some distant spot, I move my hand half an inch toward that spot, half an inch back; while doing so, I sight across the needle tip of his beak toward a reference point. Owl compensates, the tip stays almost exactly "on" that point. Does he do it by reacting to the flow of things in and out of the periphery of his vision, or can he maintain that precise distance of eye to object by depth alone? I put a three-sided box over Owl to block the cues from the periphery, and intend to move the box itself right along with the hand Owl is perched on. Owl does not cooperate; will not fixate, becomes flighty. It is not his kind of experiment. Maybe we will get back to it someday . . . not today.

Another experiment. We know that Owl tends to lean forward and nibble the finger or nose or almost anything benign which is brought toward his beak. Slowly, therefore, I move my face up to Owl's, my open eye going right toward his beak. What will Owl do? First, let's throw out any fake suspense which might be building up. I was not going to risk a scratched eye for any ornithological or behavioral data I could possibly think of. If I was curious as to what Owl would do, I was perfectly certain as to what he would *not* do. Somehow, before going through with it, I must have registered—more or less unconsciously—the bird's solicitude for our eyes. Probably it was from

the way he harassed my face a few times as I was trying to nap (think of gentle needles and less gentle tweezers) and from the way he fusses at eyebrows and eyelashes that I understood he was operating under a taboo.

The one bit of anxiety concerned Owl's unreliable vision up close. As I approached, the flesh of forehead and cheek was all bunched up ready to slam that eye shut . . . in spite of my certainty.* And, I admit, the beak began to loom larger and larger. Owl in good time turned his head away.

But he is consistent only in what he does not do. The common response, especially the first time in a series of trials, is to turn his head to the side. Several times he has seized hold of some eyebrow. I did not like it the one time he pulled at my eyelashes as if to take the eyelid too—again, he can't see well enough what he's doing at that range for that kind of trick. Often, with an almost imperceptible nod, he tucks the point of his beak into his chest. Play the game too often and he simply stays stock still: if you want to poke your eye onto the curve of his beak, that's your affair.

Now that I think on it . . . the fact that Owl closes

---

* I took no comfort from Konrad Lorenz's descriptions of his jackdaws, who would groom around his eyes in some detail. The daw and the owl, among the birds, stand apart in genealogy. The daw sees well at close range.

or half closes his eyes when I groom around his head and neck implies that maybe screech owls themselves don't trust each other's near vision any too far.

Summary of Results: I conclude that while I carried out the investigation in part to find out something about the bird, I did it mainly to have the encounter occur to be written down. Many behavioral experiments are performed in the same spirit. To court experience so as to be able to write it down—not a good way to organize one's life.

A Discussion of Tastes

Owl does not eat frogs because, in spite of their numbers around here, I won't give him one. Nor a spider. Can you imagine yourself watching while the bird tears apart and eats some large spider? Impossible. Before too long I've got to figure out why not a spider but yes to a beetle, however crackly. I note that even the most delicate person can watch a beetle or grasshopper in its last minute with Owl, but many, like me, balk at the idea of a spider. I have not, and will not, describe the uproar nor tell who took which sides when it became known Owl was to get his first mouse; but I will wonder why I am willing to feed

Owl the lovable mouse, the ugliest of caterpillars, massive beetles, even the remains of a fence lizard taken from a cat, but not a frog. Some kinds of furry caterpillar Owl will not eat because I don't know why because. Knowing some were supposed to be prickly I went so far as to brush them against my wrist, an act of raw courage, and found them indeed furry but not prickly. What bothers Owl about them, who knows? I am not going to put them to the taste test.

We have more toads than frogs. I was just barely able to bring myself to bring one to Owl, who captured and seized it up: he did not simply drop it, he whirled his head and threw it away, unharmed. And then stalked indignantly upright along behind it, as if to memorize forever the pattern of anything so bad tasting. (As if to . . . more likely, Owl's hunger moved him to track the enticing hop-hop motion, while the association between the bad taste and the look of the toad blocked a second pounce.) Personally, I am in favor of toads; I can't answer why I would offer one and not a frog.

Most birds reportedly have poor senses of smell and taste. In comparison Owl is something of a gourmet, which must seem like an outlandish claim in the light of the fact that Owl stole Grant's lucky rabbit's foot and ate it—fur, skin, nails, bones, right down to the metal clip and one last nub of bone. He may lack the dewlaps and pouting lips of the gourmet, his attention may blaze too strongly out at things, but he does have considerable tongue, sensitive bristles by the beak to help with texture, and prominent nostrils. See, he is sampling some raw liver: he stares glumly into the middle distance a while without moving, then lets it drop:* pork instead of beef. (Cat, dogs, fish, turtles—all seem to share this faint prejudice against pork liver. Any healthy appetite will overcome it, nonetheless it is there.) Even hungry, Owl is slow to eat the red earthworm, usually stops at one or two. Robin food. The great gray nightcrawler, tougher, more vigorous, he grapples zestfully with as many as he is likely to get. Maybe he likes to see himself as eagle killing a serpent. Come down from such pretensions, Owl; remember we've seen you in Jason's bowl probing around for raw meat bits among the pellets, and taking pellets if necessary. I urge Owl to learn to like the redworms, they're every bit as good as the crawlers I'm sure. Which is like the chain grocer's urging me that rock lobster is every bit as good as Maine lobster. It happens that rock lobster and redworms are both easier to obtain.

You and I, we probably prefer a lamb chop to peanuts or mints except at the times when we will

* Down the slot of the toaster? On the page of a book? Under a coil of the electric range?

take a mint or a peanut but not one more bite of chop. Of all the foods he knows in the world Owl holds most dear the mouse he has just killed, he is never more intractable than when he has one, but when not keenly hungry he may let one pass. He never refuses a moth. If the children have been successful hunters, Owl may leave the seventh grasshopper half eaten. If the eighth is something different. . . . "Well, I'm never too full for a katydid."

The gourmet is discriminating in his tastes but some of the things he enjoys may go against the public taste. I caught a few caterpillars of one of the swallowtail butterflies. An artistically gifted, demented child, not evolution, designed these things. Furthermore, they have "scent horns," bulbous bright-colored protuberances which pop out at you from a recess in the head. Owl shuts his eyes while eating them, but of course he does so for everything. Among the moths which come to the outside lights is a series of fluffy, unalert, slow-moving creatures, big of body small of wing, decorated in white, black, and orange in widely varying proportions. They have in common a smell something between marigold and geranium. Of all the eager insect-eaters which generally tenant the house— large tropical fish, turtles, transient reptiles, the doomed ducklings only Owl eats and seems to like them. The caterpillars of some of these moths eat

azaleas and viburnums. Good riddance. In listing the
insect-eaters back there, I was greatly tempted to type
in my daughter's name, and now what with all this
mention of lepidopterans in it goes: Lia, at the age of
three, ate the nourishing part of a large butterfly which
had been netted by a lepidopterist friend of mine,
while he was out getting more. She can no longer be
considered insectivorous, however.

Consider that Owl has been taken from his rightful
place in the local ecology . . . consider, but do not
regret, because that local ecology is a narrowing king-
dom yielding over to the compressed brick soil, sick
trees, and shriveled grass which the realtor leaves
behind under the flag of suburban development. We
(you, too, probably) live in what is becoming sparrow-
robin-cardinal land. Owl country is shrinking, it can
spare one citizen. And in what is left of it nearby,
aliens appear, the subsidized predators: dogs and cats.
The natives—owl and hawk, weasel and fox—owe their
continuing survival to what they prey on. Our pets
operate under no such debt or dependence. Like
human beings, some hunt expertly and avidly, some
not at all, but they all eat at home at the end of the
day. So, like deer-shooters on opening date, they scour
the environs in great numbers (and, like deer-shooters,
on rare occasions kill one another), but around the
clock and through the calendar drive out the native

predators, and decimate whatever is vulnerable to them: those that feed or nest or live on the ground or near it. When it comes to creatures like squirrels and mice, our hired scourges are almost totally incompetent. Accept my findings as if I were reporting on work by trained research people after years of census-taking in our lot: the favored rodents are doing better each year. So are the moles.

It is not because I am a bird-watcher that I regret the ripping out of owl country. (I can call myself a bird-watcher only because I can identify up to species like towhee and shrike, and own a Peterson; on the other hand, my Aunt Mildred had to tell me what it was was singing away in the oak—wood thrush.) What I regret is the exchange of forest and meadow for marigolds, telephone lines, rose gardens gleaming with disinfectant, asphalt, those damned petunia patches. Anyway, Owl has been removed from that picture, while in his stead the children and I, in trying to cater to his preferences, exert an owlish pressure on the local ecology.

Something I keep forgetting to try on Owl . . . The monarch butterfly, which is reported to be inedible, so much so that the tasty viceroy butterfly supposedly benefits from its resemblance to the former. One utterly fearless investigator I read about, however, put the monarch to the taste test—yes—and described it as just as good as any other butterfly of his experience. Perhaps in season Owl can contribute to the resolution of this issue. There's a treat—or trick—in store for you, Owl.

A List of Questions, Common or Rare, Answered or Ignored

Q. What do you feed him?
A. See pages preceding, in detail.

Q. Does he hurt?
A. No person ever.

Q. But suppose he *does* bite?

Q. Do you let him go outside?
A. No, there are *big* owls out there.

Q. Does he eat birdseed?

Q. Would you sell him?
A. No.

Q. Do they sell owls in pet shops?
A. I hope not.

Q. If you succeed in mating Owl, can we have one of the babies?

A. If you provide the mate.

Q. Since you let him fly around inside, what do you do about, ah, the droppings?

A. The best we can.

Q. Why don't you give him a real name?

A. As a general rule, I don't name a pet or captive unless it can respond to its own name and Owl responds only to whistles, hoots, other odd noises. Exceptions to the rule are: a long-gone tropical fish, a lumbering brute of striking habits named Gort after a science-fiction robot; a baleful hide-osity of a snapping turtle who had to be named Pansy. *

Q. Could he keep alive outside?

A. No doubt he could catch enough to eat. While he mistrusts strange animals, I suspect he may not mistrust them enough.

Q. If you *did* let him go, would he come back?

A. Owl is staying right here with his family.

* The turtle, then the size of a silver dollar, was brought by an ill-meaning houseguest, our old friend Smif, as a greeting. I accepted it on the condition he take the snapper back when it reached ten pounds. Pansy is getting to be a big turtle now, and I have to ask myself: Just for the satisfaction of handing back a ten-pound snapping turtle some day, is it worth it raising the beast through the days of six, seven, eight, and nine pounds?

A Survey of Attitudes
Toward One Single Screech Owl

Generally speaking: everyone who visits wants to see Owl; some visit, and bring their children, in order to see Owl; everyone who knows us knows of Owl; some people who meet us say, "Oh, you're the people with the owl." Some people want one of their own.

But, in particular. Two women are afraid of Owl, not directly, but in an edgy, phobic kind of way. One man is less than fond of Owl—"I'm afraid I identify with the mouse." Another woman dislikes all or most birds because they are "dirty and smelly." A second man, standing on the lawn, acknowledged having heard of Owl but was not curious—"I've seen owls before." Another sat with his drink while Owl, in some obscure but high excitement, winged around the room, tugged at laundry, dragged irrelevant objects along a desk—all the while the man never glancing at him until Owl made for his drink, at which the man gave a jump, one hand protectively over the glass.

Heaving into the kitchen one night under full sail in a high wind, friend Mike caught his first sight of Owl,

I guess of any owl. Mike was delighted to discover, "He looks just exactly like an *owl* . . . a classical owl."

Traveling with Owl, we find at the stops that a number of people will peer into a bird cage. Instead of finding the expected canary, they meet that blast of a glare right back at them; and they react one way or another. I am bothered, even peeved, at the occasional no-reaction, the blank, the flat incurious eyes. They don't realize they are looking at an owl.

Owl Dies

In the middle of the summer, as I was working up the last of these notes and putting them through the typewriter, the subject died. A weak appetite one stifling night—he did not bother to walk over to pick up a moth I had brought him. Unusual. Unwilling to waste what I'd caught, I gave it to him, he took it down. As occasionally he would be after a big feed, he seemed dull, sluggish. He spent his customary many minutes examining a basin of water, decided not to bathe. We left him free of his cage, told him good night.

Even the morning was hot. "Clever Owl," we said, when we saw him standing in the basin of water, where he may well have spent the night. But it was unusual. And again he seemed dull to the touch when I put him back in his cage. That afternoon Connie called me—"He's dying"—and so it was. He grew weaker as I held him upright. The claws went dead. He kept on breathing, but then, as if looking it right in the face, the open pupils shuttered down, held, and finally expanded again; a swallowing, and that was that.

The question of why—I asked our veterinarian for an autopsy. If he had any comment about the request, he kept it to himself and obliged, both macro- and microscopically, but found no cause. Unacquainted with Owl, he wondered if the bird might have been panicked by something and died from shock and beating himself against bars or glass. I pointed out how uncharacteristic that would have been, and the talk ended somewhere after the mention of pesticides— unlikely agents, since we do not use the persistent ones and rarely the others, but by their nature impossible to rule out. Owl had no last surprise for us; he was found to be a male.

I typed the last pages keeping to the convention that he was still alive. There were more pictures scheduled to be taken, more investigations to be carried out. He has left a very small blank—precisely owl-shaped—in the daily routine . . . a discontinuity which things still get caught on. And memoranda. A feather may yet swirl from a suddenly opened closet door, or come down with a book from the shelf. A fleck of lime in an angle somewhere. Punctured houseplants and page corners nipped off. We keep finding one more pellet. Will had just discovered how to make one of Owl's songs better than I could do, by blowing into his hands—he had been getting, at any rate, a higher percentage of answers—and he still calls from time to time. As I walk by any porch light, automatically I check the area for any substantial night flyer Owl might like. Cutting meat for the other animals, the knife sets for a piece bite-size for Owl. And, every now and then, someone asks about him.

We have all missed that trivial, emphatic presence. By no means a domestic creature, neither was he simply a penned wild one. Wild and tame, he showed some of the best of both. He lived less than a year and a half, we take the shortness as a rebuke of some kind, but count that odd visit a minor privilege, an emblem of the household.

**Fine works of fiction and non-fiction
available in Quality Paperback editions from Carroll & Graf**

- [ ] THE APOSTLE Sholem Asch $10.95
- [ ] THE ART OF THE MYSTERY STORY Howard Haycraft $9.95
- [ ] AUTOBIOGRAPHY Lady Diana Cooper $10.95
- [ ] AUTOBIOGRAPHIES I Sean O'Casey $10.95, cloth $21.95
- [ ] AUTOBIOGRAPHIES II Sean O'Casey $10.95, cloth $21.95
- [ ] THE BATTLE OF DIENBIENPHU Jules Roy $8.95
- [ ] THE BLAST OF WAR Harold Macmillan $12.95
- [ ] BODIES AND SOULS John Rechy $8.95, cloth $17.95
- [ ] DIARY: 1928–1957 Julian Green $9.95
- [ ] EAST RIVER Sholem Asch $8.95
- [ ] THE FORTY DAYS OF MUSA DAGH Franz Werfel $9.95
- [ ] THE FOUR HORSEMEN OF THE APOCALYPSE $8.95
      Vincente Blasco Ibañez
- [ ] GARDENS OF STONE Nicholas Proffitt   cloth $14.95
- [ ] THE GIRLS Henri de Montherlant $10.95
- [ ] GOING AWAY Clancy Sigal $9.95
- [ ] THE GOOD FATHER Peter Prince   cloth $13.95
- [ ] HERE'S WHY Colin Lambert $8.95
- [ ] HOMOSEXUALS IN HISTORY A.L. Rowse $9.95
- [ ] THE HUNTING ANIMAL Franklin Russell $7.95
- [ ] THE INHERITORS Joseph Conrad & Ford Madox Ford $7.95
- [ ] IN THE LAND OF NYX John Bowers $7.95
- [ ] INSTEAD OF A LETTER Diana Athill $7.95, cloth $15.95
- [ ] IN THE MIRO DISTRICT Peter Taylor $7.95
- [ ] JEW SUSS Lion Feuchtwanger $8.95, cloth $18.95
- [ ] JEWS WITHOUT MONEY Michael Gold $7.95
- [ ] A JOURNEY FOR OUR TIMES Harrison Salisbury $10.95
- [ ] JUSTICE AT NUREMBERG Robert Conot $10.95
- [ ] KABLOONA Gontran de Poncins $9.95
- [ ] KINGS ROW Henry Bellaman $8.95
- [ ] LATE-BLOOMING FLOWERS Anton Chekhov $8.95
- [ ] THE LONELY HUNTER: A BIOGRAPHY OF CARSON $10.95
      McCULLERS Virginia Spencer Carr
- [ ] THE LOST WEEKEND Charles Jackson $7.95
- [ ] MARCEL PROUST ON ART AND LITERATURE Marcel Proust $8.95
- [ ] THE MAURIZIUS CASE Jacob Wasserman $9.95
- [ ] MURDER FOR PLEASURE Howard Haycraft $10.95
- [ ] MYSTERIES Knut Hamsun $8.95
- [ ] NATHANAEL WEST: THE ART OF HIS LIFE Jay Martin $8.95
- [ ] THE NAZARENE Sholem Asch $10.95, cloth $21.95
- [ ] THE NOVELS AND PLAYS OF SAKI H.H. Munro $8.95
- [ ] THE OPPERMANS Lion Feuchtwanger $8.95
- [ ] A PART OF MYSELF Carl Zuckmayer $9.95

- [ ] PIERRE LOTI: THE LEGENDARY ROMANTIC Lesley Blanch $9.95
- [ ] PILGRIM'S WAY John Buchan $10.95
- [ ] PROMETHEUS: THE LIFE OF BALZAC Andre Maurois $11.95
- [ ] PROUST: PORTRAIT OF A GENIUS Andre Maurois $10.95
- [ ] ROMANCE Joseh Conrad & Ford Madox Ford $8.95
- [ ] RUSSIA AT WAR: 1941–1945 Alexander Werth $15.95
- [ ] THE SABRES OF PARADISE Lesley Blanch $9.95
- [ ] SEXUAL AWARENESS Barry & Emily McCarthy $9.95
- [ ] SINGAPORE GRIP J.G. Farrell $10.95
- [ ] SITUATIONAL ANXIETY H.J. Freudenberger $8.95
- [ ] SONYA: THE LIFE OF COUNTESS TOLSTOY Anne Edwards $8.95
- [ ] STALINGRAD Theordore Plievier $8.95
- [ ] THE STORY OF SAN MICHELE Axel Munthe $8.95
- [ ] SUCCESS Lion Feuchtwanger $10.95
- [ ] SUMMER IN WILLIAMSBURG Daniel Fuchs $8.95
- [ ] THREE CITIES Sholem Asch $10.95
- [ ] THREE PLUS ONE EQUALS BILLIONS Allan Sloan $8.95
- [ ] TOLSTOY: TALES OF COURAGE & CONFLICT Charles Neider, ed. $10.95
- [ ] THE TRIANGLE FIRE Leon Stein $7.95
- [ ] VIRGINIE: HER TWO LIVES John Hawkes $7.95
- [ ] THE WAY OF A TRANSGRESSOR Negley Farson $9.95
- [ ] THE WILDER SHORES OF LOVE Lesley Blanch $8.95
- [ ] WORK WITH PASSION Nancy Anderson cloth $15.95
- [ ] YOU MUST KNOW EVERYTHING Isaac Babel $8.95

Available at fine bookstores everywhere

To order direct from the publishers please send check or money order includ-
ing the price of the book plus $1.75 per title for postage and handling.
N.Y. State Residents please add 8¼% sales tax.

Carroll & Graf Publishers, Inc.
260 Fifth Avenue, New York, N.Y. 10001